Assertiveness Training

The complete workbook for women and men to learn outstanding assertiveness strategies. Change your behavior, stand up for yourself, and reap the benefits that will 10x your confidence.

KEITH COLEMAN

and audio unless express consent of the Publisher is provided beforehand. Any additional rights reserved.

Furthermore, the information that can be found within the pages described forthwith shall be considered both accurate and truthful when it comes to the recounting of facts. As such, any use, correct or incorrect, of the provided information will render the Publisher free of responsibility as to the actions taken outside of their direct purview. Regardless, there are zero scenarios where the original author or the Publisher can be deemed liable in any fashion for any damages or hardships that may result from any of the information discussed herein.

Additionally, the information in the following pages is intended only for informational purposes and should thus be thought of as universal.

As befitting its nature, it is presented without assurance regarding its prolonged validity or interim quality. Trademarks that are mentioned are done without written consent and can in no way be considered an endorsement from the trademark holder.

Table of Contents

INTRODUCTION

Assertiveness is a great skill to build, and the tools and techniques gone over in this book will help you to bolster your ability to act assertively, leading with more confidence, more power, and a greater self-image.

It doesn't matter whether you are non-assertive because you lack confidence or if you simply do not like conflict. Assertiveness training can help you to better express yourself in all walks of life.

Here we will delve into the causes and effects of assertive or non-assertive modes of conduct. Assertiveness usually stems from confidence and a desire to meet some end, while non-assertiveness usually stems from the desire to solve problems without direct conflict. Before trying to be more assertive in everyday life, we do need to analyze the roots of our interpersonal problems so that we are actually solving problems with assertive action, a theme that this book touches on repeatedly.

Assertiveness requires confidence. We cannot rightfully stick up for our thoughts and beliefs if we do not have any real confidence in them. When we doubt the validity of our own viewpoints, they tend to become less and less valid. Confidence is here defined as the belief in one's self and in one's own ability to succeed. This belief causes us to go through life feeling assured that we are good enough to do all of the things, things that we want to do, and that we will not fail in our efforts to succeed. Self-doubt and limiting beliefs are two of the greater antagonists of success, so if we want to find rewarding lives for ourselves, we need to remain confident in our ability to succeed.

Within this book you will learn techniques to bolster your confidence, ways to better express how you truly feel to yourself and others, some of the ways by which you can lose assertiveness and what to do once it has been lost, how to assert yourself when put in bad situations, how to actually externalize your thoughts in assertive manners, conversational techniques that better assertiveness, and hypothetical examples of assertiveness used in dialogue, including examples of when an assertive person does not get his or her way, as is often the case.

Please Enjoy!

Chapter One

How To Stop Lying To Yourself And Communicate How You Feel Towards Others In Your Life

Assertiveness is a social skill that needs to be developed like any other. This skill requires certain communication abilities, which enable us to effectively express our own positions, boundaries, wants, and needs to others. We should allegorize this skill to a muscle, one that needs to be exercised in order to become big and strong. Assertive people are those who can stick up for themselves without offending or squashing the opinions of others. This skill requires us to walk in a fine balance, placed between meeting our own needs and respecting those of others.

One of the biggest enemies, if not the arch-enemy, of assertiveness, is self-deception. All too often, we convince ourselves that we are fine with the way things are, simply to avoid making waves and upsetting people. This often causes us to spend prolonged periods of our lives, failing to address the issues that cause us the most concern. A lack of assertiveness does not just make us weaker as individuals; it completely controls our lives, forcing us to simply sit back and placidly accept the often grim realities that we are met with.

In order to become more assertive about our positions and needs, we must first define clearly what these positions and needs are. Assertive people have no doubt as to where they stand on the issues they face and know exactly what they need out of life. A passive person will stay in a living arrangement that causes him or her grief for years because such a person has no idea of how he or she really feels about the arrangement, nor what it is that he or she needs in order to be happy with a living arrangement. An assertive person, on the other hand, can pinpoint exactly what it is that is causing the harm and knows what he or she would prefer instead.

Cognitively, an assertive person generally feels much less stress than a passive person does. Not only are assertive people much better at coping with anxious thoughts than others are, but they also experience less of them overall, presumably because of the added sense of control that they feel over their own lives. The firmness divorced from rudeness with which assertive people react to people and situations is what allows them to find their golden mean between aggression and passivity. Along this behavioral path the assertive person goes through life with more confidence and higher self-esteem, never being afraid to voice his or her opinions or to try to influence others to see things his or her way.

Conflict is a predicate to relationships. We cannot become invested in any way with other people without eventually experiencing some form of conflict. When we find ourselves in conflict with others we have two basic options: we can neglect our own point of view and simply accept that of the other, or we can clearly and respectfully voice our point of view in a way that we see befitting towards the purpose of solving the issue causing the conflict. Here is where a fair amount of pragmatism is needed; when we voice opinions without the purposiveness of solving the conflict, we are bound to solve nothing and possibly offend the other person. Conflict should not be indulged in; that is to say, it should not be had merely for its own sake as a pastime. When we experience disagreements with others, we should conduct ourselves in a way that enables us to voice our perspective, and that hopefully solves the issues underlying the disagreement.

Assertiveness is positively correlated to a greater sense of agency, lower rates of anxiety and depression, and overall better relationships. This social skill is often conflated with aggression, but it differs from aggression in that assertive people do not assert themselves simply to bully or antagonize other people. They typically do not have any behavioral issues and usually do not lash out at others. Being assertive, as opposed to being aggressive, is more about saving one's own items from fire and less about starting fires.

Traditionally, a person must meet two criteria in order to be deceiving him or her self: 1. The self-deceiver must hold contradictory beliefs and, 2. He or she must intentionally hold a belief thought or known to be false. Sometimes we have so much difficulty reconciling the issues in our lives that we force ourselves to hold on to false beliefs, usually out of a want for comfort and/or control.

Rationalization is one psychological coping mechanism that we use, either consciously or unconsciously, to explain or justify polarizing feeling or behaviors in logical and rational ways. This process can cause us to continue to subscribe to false beliefs on the pretext that our subscriptions are based on logical and rational thinking patterns. We can argue for the validity of near stance using logical acrobatics, and rationalization causes us to genuinely believe our own arguments, however improbable the beliefs for which we are arguing happen to be.

The basis of rationalization is usually found in socialization, fear, personal biases, and cognitive repression. We can either rationalize positively or negatively, meaning that we can choose to perceive negative situations positively and visa-versa. No matter the causes of rationalization, or the direction in which we are rationalizing, this process is still seen as a coping mechanism, a thinking pattern that is not obedient to reality and therefore does not necessarily help us.

Sometimes our attachments to these faulty beliefs are emotional in their onset. It is when we are experiencing our most salient experiences that we, therefore, become most susceptible to self-deception. Someone who is experiencing no issues at the present moment has much less likelihood of falling into self-deceptive thinking patterns because the individual has no need to convince him or herself of false beliefs in order to rationalize reality. When reality is bearable, our minds can accept the truth at face value. It is when reality becomes too painful to deal with that we fall into self-deception.

We all deceive ourselves from time to time. Self-deception is all too easy of a trap to fall into, but what is not so easy is reversing its effects once it has made its way into our thinking patterns. Mitigating self-deceit and limiting beliefs is so difficult because once these patterns are established in our minds, it becomes almost impossible to differentiate thoughts produced by these patterns from more rational ones. When trying to separate our own personal truths from our fictions, we inevitably either disregard some truths as falsehoods or exalt some falsehoods as truths. In this way, self-deception causes our entire integrated knowledge structures to become unreliable, with no boundaries separating truth from untruth.

We can, however, clearly and concisely go over the more constrictive beliefs that we hold in an effort to ascertain where truths are and where falsehood stands. When thoughts that we have stick out to us as being divorced from reality (at least seemingly) we should take note of them, thinking on them over critically, trying to find other more rational thoughts to replace them and bring us closer to the light of truth. If we do not take the time to analyze these more faulty thinking patterns, they are bound to take over our lives, forcing us away from the truth that is always right in front of our eyes.

Our emotions and the thought contents related to them are our top priority psychologically. These are what make us who we are, and are the only things that truly guide us through life and make it worth living. If we cannot be honest about these emotions, and cannot express them to ourselves and others, then we are missing out on leading honest lives. This honesty is, however, much more easily spoken about than achieved.

In order to be more honest with ourselves and others, we have first to recognize that we are not necessarily wrong for feeling the emotions that we do, no matter what they happen to be. While our emotions may, at times, be irrational and out of proportion to the scenario at large, these feelings are an integral part of ourselves and demand our attention. If a person is angry at the amount of traffic he is in then throwing his cup of coffee out of the window is probably not appropriate, but his intuition to do so caused by his temporary anger should not be ignored. We are not always the greatest judges of how to react to experiences, but we are usually serving as legislators of our own emotions, so we will always do well to hear out what these emotions are trying to tell us.

Authenticity and straightforwardness are two incredibly becoming traits in a person. No matter how much people are put off by our frankness, it is that frankness that allows us to function authentically through life in the first place, so it is not to be disregarded or eliminated. Being nice and agreeable are two very charming characteristics, but they are not always called for and are not always the best ways to be about things. Sometimes allowing ourselves to be as honest and as frank as possible will show that we are much more disagreeable and unpleasant to be around than we initially thought we were, but there is nothing wrong with disagreeable modes when they are necessary, and in order to truly feel comfortable in our own skin we have to integrate these darker sides of our character. Doing so frees us from our shackles of politeness and allows us to make further progress psychologically, but neglecting to do so only leads to a lack of self-acceptance and an inability to express the more "honest" parts of ourselves.

Authenticity refers to the degree to which a person's actions are congruent to his or her desires or beliefs, regardless of any external factors. Someone whose actions diverge in their purposiveness from his or her own beliefs or desires is said to be inauthentic, while someone who acts according to his or her own maxims is said to be authentic. Authenticity found in action is separated from the concept of external influences here because the authenticity in our actions is only measured by the comparative contents of our beliefs and desires. The concept of authenticity could here be expressed in the age-old adage "know thyself," but should rather be extended to "be thyself."

When we base our actions off of the purposes and ends of external factors, we cheat ourselves out of our own agency, which is usually limited in the first place in of itself. Inauthenticity in the sense of working simply for the needs of others is useless in a twofold manner: not only does it not fulfill our own needs, but it usually does not fully appease those who we are working for the betterment of, since people are never satisfied with any given amount of help that they may receive from another.

Many postmodernist thinkers assert that we are merely cultural constructs, whose thoughts and actions are based on the general will of those around us. While the degree to which this view is valid is debatable, what can not be argued against is that we are constantly influenced by those around us, for better or worse. This is why we have to consider our own wishes first, or else those of everyone else will take over our headspace, and perhaps our own purposive actions if we are not careful about what we are spending our time on.

Chapter Two

Inspiring Confidence In Yourself Through Assertiveness

Assertiveness requires confidence. We cannot rightfully stick up for our thoughts and beliefs if we do not have any real confidence in them. When we doubt the validity of our own viewpoints, they tend to become less and less valid. Confidence is here defined as the belief in one's self and in one's own ability to succeed. This belief causes us to go through life feeling assured that we are good enough to do all of the things that we want to do and that we will not fail in our efforts to succeed. Self-doubt and limiting beliefs are two of the greater antagonists of success, so if we want to find rewarding lives for ourselves, we need to remain confident in our ability to succeed.

Confidence, like any other personality trait, is best sustained within a golden mean. Having too much or too little belief in one's ability to succeed skews one's perceptions of what he or she can actually achieve if the effort is put in. It is within our nature to incline towards overconfidence, constantly overestimating our abilities and subsequently running into unforeseen problems and failing in areas in which we did not predict we would have issues. Some of us, on the other hand, is bent more towards diffidence, presuming that they have less ability than they in fact do, and subsequently avoiding or talking themselves out of tasks and activities that they could show aptitude in.

If overconfidence leads to being blindsided by our own ineptitudes, and under-confidence leads to our missing out on opportunities that could have potentially made our lives better and more fulfilling, then it becomes clear that we need to make clear, concerted efforts to keep our egos within healthy and realistic boundaries. Maintaining this more healthy level of confidence betters both our self-image and our reputation. People find others with normal confidence more trustworthy, as they are better at ascertaining what they can do in certain situations and what they are unable to do. We also make much better first impressions when we are more realistic about ourselves. People find moderately confident people more approachable and realistic.

In order to better our self-confidence, we do not need to be overly optimistic or to cut ourselves short regarding our abilities. The only outlook that will manage our ego is one that converges with reality, praising ourselves when we are in the right, and being honest with ourselves when we are in the wrong. Others will put more faith in us not when we are arrogant about our own abilities, but when they see that we have a clear concept of what those abilities are. Many modern people learn a little about everything and go on to deem themselves capable of anything, but a truly confident person knows that he or she is limited in the scope of ability and acts accordingly. To take on things that are outside of our abilities simply for the sake of bolstering our egos is to lay the groundwork for a loss of faith in our own abilities, both in ourselves and in others.

Confidence has been said to be found at the core of four other variables: hope, self-efficacy, resilience, and optimism. Confidence bolsters a sense of hope in that it shows one what needs to be done in order to meet an objective and how to do it. It affects self-efficacy in that it shows one that certain tasks can, in fact, be completed. Resilience is gained through confidence by the belief that one can overcome any of the obstacles in one's way, and optimism is also gained through confidence as confidence offers one a much more positive outlook on things.

Without confidence, our latent potential can never truly unfold. Always doubting whether or not he or she can perform certain tasks, the diffident person simply puts all assignments off out of fear of failure. Self-confident people, on the other hand, jump into tasks without worrying what the final outcomes might be. It's not that confident people never fail; it's only that they do not let the prospect of failure deter them from trying to achieve their goals. Confidence allows people to make any attempts that they have in mind, without fear of failure or the dismissal of others.

Confidence is positively linked with a number of crucial lifetime parameters such as workplace satisfaction, academic performance, and overall life satisfaction. People who are more confident usually get better jobs, more frequent raises, better grades, and tend to make more money. The phenomenon here is not that confident people are overall more adept or intelligent than others; it is that they are less afraid to work towards their goals and resultantly tend to be rewarded much more for their efforts than others. Confidence is not an indication of greater talents; it is only an outlook that tends to get people into much better living situations.

Self-regulation is also increased in more confident individuals. The more confident a person is, the more he or she is willing to change the things that he or she wants to. Diffident people are much more timorous when it comes to enacting personal changes. For this reason, they will often spend much of their lives doing things and living in situations that they do not enjoy simply because they are too afraid to change things around and do not always know what they would rather have happen. As a result of this increased sense of self-regulation more confident people are much better with things like problem-solving and planning ahead because they have clearer visions of what they want to have happen, as well as added confidence in their abilities to enact the changes that they deem necessary.

Confidence begets assertiveness and visa versa. When we feel more confident in the validity of our own viewpoints, we tend to have much less trouble voicing those viewpoints. The perception that our opinions are just as valid as any others, drive us to voice them without concern. A person who is confident in his scientific abilities, for example, is much more likely to voice his opinions concerning new developments in astrophysics, while a more diffident person would be more inclined to shoot down his own opinions on the matter. Without confidence, all of our stances become flimsy and chaotic, legislated largely by the viewpoints of others around us.

Increased awareness of personal rights is the first objective in most forms of assertiveness training. With this increased awareness, people gain the capacity to stick up for themselves with the knowledge of what is within their rights and what is not. Without this awareness, people run the risk of being put back into place if they happen to exceed their rights. With this risk factor accounted for, people naturally become much more diffident and are likely to let others convince them that they have fewer rights than they in fact do. When people do not know their positive and negative rights, these apparent rights can be given to them by people who do not have their own best interests in mind. Without knowledge of our rights, we cannot truly stick up for ourselves because we do not know when we are within these rights and when we are without them.

The next objective of assertiveness training is the differentiation made between non-assertiveness and assertiveness. By non-assertiveness here we mean either aggressiveness or passiveness. Picking fights with and bullying others could be deemed aggressiveness. Never asserting one's self and or avoiding all confrontation at any costs could be considered passiveness. Both of these modes of conduct are extremely damaging to us because they are either out of line with how we truly feel in certain situations or are indicative of poor means of expressing frustrations and worries. Assertiveness training is here used to separate the wheat from the chaff, with all examples of loutishness and aggression, as well as all examples of cowardice and meekness, being eliminated.

The differentiation between assertiveness and passive aggressiveness need also be made in assertiveness training. Passive aggressiveness is most commonly defined as the pattern of indirect refusal to the requests and demands of other people as well as the avoidance of direct forms of confrontation. This mode of conduct is used by people who are desirous of getting their ways without confronting others directly. It is not an advisable mode of conduct because it often manifests poor communications among people and usually does not solve the interpersonal issues at hand. This form of aggressiveness differs from direct aggressiveness only in that it is indirect; both have the capacity to do great harm to those who are worked against.

The final objective in most forms of assertiveness training is the learning of both verbal and nonverbal assertiveness skills. The learning of verbal assertiveness skills could include thinking of ways in which we could make our opinions more direct and more pragmatic in times of conflict, going through individual examples of situations that may demand greater assertiveness on our parts. Nonverbal assertiveness skills deal mostly with body language. The use of eye contact, as well as the broadening of the chest and the arching of the back, are usually the greatest things that we can do in the way of looking more assertive to others. Without learning these skills, all of the other points of assertiveness training can fall by the wayside, so this final step is likely the most important.

With this training, our confidence is bound to increase. Once we have learned our rights, we become much better able to stick up for ourselves. Once we have learned the differences among assertive, nonassertive, passive-aggressive, and aggressive communication styles we know, for the most part, how to communicate what we need out of others as the situation demands. Finally, once we can communicate in assertive manners both verbally and nonverbally people will start to see us in a much different light, taking more heed of what we say and how we act and respecting us much more.

Confident and assertive people are good boundary setters and tend to respect the boundaries of others well. Cooperation among people who are more assertive is much easier than it is with other people. This is because more assertive people are much more likely to have their own needs met in the first place, giving them much more leeway to deal with others because they have much to offer and can afford to lose a little. When people's demands are generally met, their overall demands tend to decrease in number, and they become more satisfied with what they have rather than expecting with nervous anticipation more and more. There is also less incentive to knit pick and to glower over middle ground among people who are more satisfied. Pettiness involving what someone has control over tends to dissipate when people have control over more things, so control giving assertive attributes become some of the greatest terminators of pettiness over superfluities.

Assertive people typically have a much easier time establishing and maintaining meaningful relationships with others, which causes their confidence to skyrocket. Knowing that many people are on his or her side, the assertive person goes through life ready and willing to voice his or her opinions and beliefs with the reassurance that others will stand behind what is said. These people are also naturally better anger managers, as assertiveness itself is the editing and encapsulation of aggressive and angry modes of thought. This is a further counterpart to confidence, as the assertive person can go through life knowing that no matter what happens, he or she will be able to control his or her emotions in a respectful and mature manner, even when incredibly frustrated.

Some of the most common techniques used for bettering assertiveness are the broken record technique, fogging, negative assertion, negative inquiry, and I statements. The broken record technique consists of repeating refusals or assertion for as long as they are ignored by others. Fogging consists of agreeing with some limited truth or just a part of what the antagonist is saying. A negative inquiry is the requesting of more and more specific pieces of criticism. A negative assertion is agreeing with criticisms put forth while still pressing forward on a specific demand. Finally, I statements are used to express one's own personal opinions or beliefs without asserting judgments towards those who the expressions are meant for.

Confidence is an intrinsic value which can only be supplemented or diminished according to criteria imposed by the holder's own power of judgment. When we feel confident about our knowledge or our abilities concerning a certain subject, we feel so because we have determined that we have successfully fulfilled obligations of skill or competence that have only been assigned to us by our own power of judgment. We are the only legislators of our confidence in this respect. While the opinions of others concerning us have an effect on our self-perceptions, it is only the fulfillment of our own personal standards that will rationalize our own confidence or diffidence. Here we become the architects of our own lives, building their own foundations, and choosing their contents. It is only through our own self-perceptions that we can feel confident in our abilities and knowledge.

Assertiveness is such a great counterpart to confidence because it is only though assertiveness that we can truly and rationally express all of our opinions and viewpoints to others. While we may be the ultimate determiners of our own confidence, we still seek out confirmation of the validity of our viewpoints in others to get a more objective stance on what we are thinking and feeling. While a one-party stance on any given matter can be perfectly rational and correct when more parties confirm the validity of the stance in question, the confidence of the prognosticator tends to increase. This interpersonal communication with the aim of validation of beliefs is a great proponent of confidence that can only be properly commiserated with a certain degree of assertiveness.

If our confidence is dependent upon our own self-perceptions, legislated by the merits or demerits that we perceive in our own viewpoints, then the aspiration of assertiveness is also dependent upon these self-perceptions. The aspiration of assertiveness can therefore only be achieved once we have established and met the criteria necessary for the establishment of confidence. Once this aspiration of assertiveness has been achieved, we can then formulate what we need to assert ourselves concerning. A rational and valid aspiration of assertiveness is not one caused by the perceived impotence and or ineptitude in one's self, but it is instead brought forth by the perceived necessity to make certain changes in one's life for the betterment of the individual and perhaps also of others.

In other words, the assertion is rationally necessitated by a purposiveness coupled with the concept of a purpose; in order to make a rational assertion there has to be a teleological judgment concerning its contents in place, that is to say, a judgment that assigns a purpose to a purposiveness. The issue with more weak-willed and diffident assertions is that they do not serve a purpose, and are instead initiated by irrational and limiting beliefs. To practice assertiveness with no concept of pragmatism in mind, with the simple aim of protecting or bolstering one's own ego is to work without confidence towards goals that are not purposive towards the betterment of the individual will.

Whatever may inspire confidence within the individual is subjective, but there are certain commonalities concerning the establishment of a better self-image within most people. In this way, nature provides answers in the regularity of its contingent constituents. Most people are endowed with a greater sense of self-confidence when they fell assured of the validity of their viewpoints, and when they are assured of their own self-worth and esteem through fortunate or just turns of events. When we are incessantly contradicted for seemingly no reason or are faced with adversities outside of the realm of what we deem just, our confidence in ourselves tends to wane, even though these happenings may not always be justified by our thoughts or actions. When, on the other hand, we are experiencing fortune, or are revered or commiserated by others as a result of our expressed stances, we tend to feel more and more confident in our thoughts and abilities, whether we are in fact deserving of the good fortune that is being bestowed upon us.

Almost anyone with any theory of mind is bound to have very valuable ideas that can be of great use to others. Truth can be found in virtually any given person, regardless of how others may view the individual. This truth that we all hold justifies the aspiration to the assertion, as we all have some valid viewpoints to offer others. With this half promise of reception in others, we can feel more comfortable asserting our ideas to others if the anxiety that others may not hear us out is held. As we all know, no one makes accurate statements at all times, so there need not be any fear of showing ignorance to others. It is incredibly freeing to accept our own ignorance because doing so keeps us in line with realistic standards that allow that we are not always going to be in the right.

Rational assertions beget confidence in that they offer our rational judgments and ideas to others, expressing our more realistic thinking patterns. While the trains of cognition underlying these assertions may sometimes lead to inaccurate or low-resolution conclusions, posterity will usually only hold the grain in which these assertions traveled, for whatever it is worth. When expressed, correct assertions become declarations, and incorrect ones become mere blunders. When not expressed, both correct and incorrect assertions remain mere mind fodder.

Chapter Three

Why We Sometimes Lack Assertiveness

Assertiveness is a rare personality trait for diverse reasons. Everyone has the capacity for assertiveness within them and does display this trait from time to time, but there are also times in which we can not muster up any assertiveness within ourselves whatsoever. Most people careen either towards aggressiveness or passivity with occasional references towards assertiveness, but very few stay assertive throughout most situations they experience.

Assertiveness, or a lack thereof, can work within a causal loop to diminish confidence and self-esteem, further damaging our capacity for assertiveness in the future. A lack of confidence and self-esteem is probably the number one reason why people are not as assertive as they should be. There are very few factors that affect assertiveness more so than these tend to do.

The roles we adopt also play a large part in determining our levels of assertiveness throughout the grand scale of our interactions. If we take up primarily passive and subordinate roles in most or all of the places that we go, including work and home, then our attitudes and demeanors when dealing with other people are bound to reflect that. The way we interact with one or a few people tend to trickle out and to affect the interactions that we have with all others as our behavioral patterns establish themselves, and we adapt to our sociological environment. The same is true for the more dominant roles that we take on. Our characters are shaped heavily by our roles within the structures we find ourselves in.

Our work lives constitute most of our waking hours as adults, so those of us who are put into more subordinate roles at work, are bound to develop the most passivity in our dispositions. If people see us merely as cogs in their own machines, that is what we are bound to become unless we work against those people or at least work within our own self-interests. All too many people let their own work lives become unbalanced by the needs of others because they are too afraid and too diffident to assert themselves with those they work with. A certain degree of obedience to one's superiors is always necessary for holding down a job, but where people run into trouble is when establishing boundaries that they need to be respected in order to function properly at work. People tend to debase themselves far too much in their interactions with their superiors. The fear of reproach or even of punishment is a great deterrent to people who wish to assert their own needs, but authority figures are humans just like the rest of us and are usually reasonable when addressing the concerns of those who work for them. Keeping in mind that while we may not hold the same stature as these people do in the workplace, but are still their equals in life, will make addressing our concerns with our superiors much easier and less anxiety provoking.

We determine our own roles in life, within reason. By this, it means that we decide where we want to go and what we want to do. We are usually not necessarily compelled to act or to comply by external forces. When we see certain roles as having adverse or damaging effects on us, we can either abandon these roles, establish their new boundaries, or simply comply with their current ones. We can not always abandon the roles that we have, as sometimes we are forced into things that are simply out of our control. At other times this proves to be our best option though, due to the fact that sometimes our desertion has the greatest benefit not just for ourselves but also for all others. While conforming to roles that we are not desirous of may seem to calm the waters initially, this over conformity manifests resentment over time, resentment towards ourselves, others, and the overall situation at hand.

Typically, establishing new boundaries with the purpose of making our roles more agreeable/livable to us is the best bet that we have. This is the only option that we have that requires assertiveness, so we can not afford to not utilize it. To assume that everything is always just going to fall into place perfectly is disobedient to reality; it is only with editing and negotiated dialogues that we can work towards more healthy and sustainable roles for ourselves. What may work at first will not always necessarily work. Similarly, many of the things that seem detrimental to us at first, become the most desirable possible circumstances once we assert ourselves and establish our boundaries.

Finally, compliance with undesirable standards should only be met within dire straits, and does not precipitate long term fulfillment or life success. This compliance can at times be necessary when we simply have no other options on hand but is usually needless. There is always a part of us that would rather simply comply with harmful living conditions than assert its own needs. While this part of us is usually a rational one that needs to be reconciled with all others, we should view this part of ourselves as what it truly is: the part of us that remains a slave. Sometimes we are put into circumstances that are completely out of our control, but at other times it is only our own ineptitude and failure to take life by its reigns that forces us into the situations that harm us the most. It is better to fail miserably in trying to escape a bad situation and make something of ourselves than it is to pigeonhole ourselves into compliance with standards that we disapprove of.

As far as the sexes are concerned, it is the general consensus that women are typically more passive than men. For this reason, it is likely preferable for women to err on the side of over-assertiveness as to overcome many of the more aggressive and possibly chauvinistic men that they are bound to encounter. Without this adaption of temperament, many more passive women are bound to be stepped all over by more assertive people.

Past experiences (or better, our reactions to past experiences) are great predictors of how assertively we are bound to react to certain situations. If an individual has adopted more subordinate roles in the past, the same types of roles are bound to be adopted in the future. The same is true for one who has adopted leadership roles; he or she is likely to remain a leader in the future. People are naturally resistant to change, what more, chance often happens to put people in the same situations over and over again throughout the course of their lives, so it should come as no surprise that most people would spend the bulk of their lives adopting or being forced into the same types of roles again and again.

Stress is another key determinant of assertive behavior. There are two usually reactions to stress concerning interpersonal relationships: passivity and aggression. Passivity is often found in the actions of people under stress because when we are under too much stress, we feel less in control of our own lives. This causes us to either simply let events unfold as they will, taking no efforts to influence them, or to do the reverse and to become compensatorily aggressive when dealing with others. The perceived lack of control resultant of high levels of stress causes us to act unnaturally and to communicate our opinions in very unhealthy manners.

Stressors put our minds into fight or flight mode. In this mode, our brains work very quickly and almost hastily at times. Often, when we are stressed, connections are made, and viewpoints that are come to, that are irrational and have no basis in reality. The worst part of this happening is probably that we are usually aware of our own in correctitude under these circumstances. Knowing that we are under stress and not knowing how to deal with our problems properly, we often become vindictively course or self sacrificially passive under these circumstances. In this way, assertiveness becomes easier for those with less stress, which is why those with more would benefit more from assertiveness training of some sort.

Here is one thread through which the age-old debate weaves itself: are people naturally more or less assertive by nature or by nurture. If we analyze ourselves and deem that we were born near either end of the spectrum, it becomes clear that we should strive to be more or less assertive as our characters imply. There are no known inborn proclivities towards assertiveness, passivity, or aggression, so while some people may seem certain ways by nature, we cannot typecast based on what we perceive others to be born with or without. A greater concern here is how to better our assertiveness. This involves acting in the opposite manner than we usually do, as no one is all the way assertive, passive, or aggressive, and everyone exists on a temperamental spectrum which allows them to adapt with changing circumstances and roles.

Assertiveness is all about how we, as individuals, treat the rights of others and of ourselves. Passivity concerning either class of these rights leads to these rights being trampled on. With no defenders of our liberties, we tend to lose every single one. Aggression, on the other hand, often causes the aggressor to become the one doing the trampling. Rights can only be respected and kept when their keepers are assertive about their boundaries and needs. To be loutish is to exceed one's rights, but to be passive is never firmly to establish these rights in the first place.

In order to properly assert one's self, one needs to be aware of his or her own rights. The most basic assertive rights that each individual is entitled to are the following:

The right to express values, opinions, feelings, and beliefs

What is commonly said about the first American amendment could also be said for this interpersonal right: that it is the right on which all others are based upon and made possible by. Aside from values, opinions, feelings, and beliefs, there is little else that we have to express to others, and even less that is worth expressing. Without this right, we would not be able to assert how we truly feel about things, which would make any valuable form of communication impossible, as it is only truth that makes practical and theoretical communication worthwhile.

The right to change one's mind

Things change, and we have both a right and sometimes an obligation to change our minds with the happenings of the times. Without this fundamental right, our ability to adapt is hindered, and with that hinderance comes death.

The right to make decisions

This right is the one that allows us to establish new boundaries for ourselves in the situations that we find ourselves in. Without this right, our faculty of judgment has no purposiveness because none of our analysis can bring about change when our will cannot be compelled to initiate changes. This right extends to every situation we find ourselves in, including those in which we seem to have no power to influence our own external circumstances.

The right to say "I do not understand" and/or "I do not know."

We are allowed ignorance even when this ignorance bothers others. To never use these phrases is to lie to ourselves and others.

The right to say "no" without feelings of guilt

It has been said by more than one influential person that the difference between successful and unsuccessful people are that successful people say no to almost everything. Without allowing ourselves to use this word, we are bound to force ourselves into obligations that we do not desire and ones that do not help us. There is nothing disrespectful or even disagreeable in saying "no" simply and calmly.

The right to be non-assertive

We also hold the right to be non-assertive. This means that we do not always have to act assertively.

The right to personal freedom and to be one's own self

This is likely the broadest right of all the ones listed here. We maintain a right to be and to represent our most authentic selves. This right is necessary because we are all doing this necessarily at any given point in time, but what is being implied here is that our own personal characters have a right to act as autonomous stand-alone, ones that are given preference over any false or inaccurate conceptualizations of our characters projected outward into the world. We have a right to determine and act upon our own self-interests as well; a right included within the concept of individual sovereignty. Authenticity is a broad concept in that its manifestations are subject and discursive, varying from person to person. This right does protect personal authenticity in all cases, though.

The right to privacy, or to be on one's own and independent

We maintain a right to our personal privacy and to live without any others. We cannot allow others to invade our privacy, or else we will have no sense of escape from them. Without some sense of escape from others or at least some space that we can keep all to ourselves, we tend to react like dogs cornered in cages with others, biting and growling at all those who we are forced to be around. We are also not necessarily compelled to live around others. If we choose to live by ourselves, virtually no one can compel us to do otherwise. We are autonomous actors who choose who we associate with and who have a right to personal space.

Privacy is a difficult concept; while the only truly private area we have is our own headspace, not even this area is free from the interjections and inquiries of others. To keep others away from our own property is within our rights though, as personal property is protected by a right to exclusion in most (if not all) countries. Our right to privacy does extend beyond property though; we also have a right to exclude others from our personal lives and to refuse to be around them if we so choose to do.

The rights mentioned above are shared by all people, so we can exercise any number of these, but we should also be aware that others can do the same. If we do not respect the rights of others, then we are not living by universalisable moral maxims, and, as a result, cannot expect our own rights to be respected. A distinction between positive and negative rights should also be made: we all have rights concerning what we can and cannot do. We tend to consider more negative rights for others and positive ones for ourselves, that is to say, we look more for what other people can be prohibited from doing and for what we are allowed to do and less for what we are prohibited from doing and for what others are allowed to do. Everyone has the same positive and negative rights, so our own prohibitions are shared by all, as well as our own allowances.

Assertiveness does not entail that all of our wishes are going to be automatically granted to us. The development of this skill will make others much more likely to receive our messages, but this does not necessarily indicate that our desires will always be met. This is just another factor that goes into the manifestations of our assertive tendencies. Though, truly assertive people know that they will not always get their way, and shape their conduct accordingly. In this way, assertiveness becomes less about expected outcomes and more about the extent to which we can influence these outcomes if we try. Here maturity is in order, in the ability to see that we are not always likely to get our own ways.

Since we can usually not give outright directives to our equals, assertiveness relies heavily on the practices of cooperation and negotiation. These practices are virtually the only ones that ensure that no parties involved within a conflict get their rights stepped on and that all parties have their voices heard and are able to work according to their own wills. Interpersonal needs are heavily reciprocal: others have just as many needs as we do. A categorical imperative would assume that we have to be willing to open up talks with others if we are to expect others to do the same.

Negotiation requires the ability to see the perspectives of others. One-sided negotiations are only seen where one party is backed into a corner, and cannot justly be called negotiations. The most effective way to get the most out of a negotiation is to convince the other party(s) that they are getting what they want. This does not entail lying to or misleading others; it only requires us to give a little to others for whatever it is that we want in return.

Assertiveness is a form of cooperation. It is, in part, the ability to work with others to meet one's own ends. We work towards our own purposes first when cooperating, and when the purposes of others present themselves, we should hear these purposes out while still looking out for ourselves above all else. If a person goes to a superior at work hoping for a raise and is met with a request to do extra work, it becomes clear that the two can cooperate by the inferior working extra for the raise. Without this cooperation, it is not clear that either party would get its own ends met.

Chapter Four

Maintaining Assertiveness In Uncomfortable Situations

Where we tend to lack assertiveness the most is in the more uncomfortable situations that we find ourselves in. Making matters worse, it is in these situations that we need to be our most assertive. Assertiveness is of limited value if we cannot hone in and use it where it really matters. These more ungainly and discomforting situations we are met with are the ones in which we should practice assertiveness the most because doing so will grant us more power and control in times of crisis.

The huge conflicts are usually not the ones in which we lose the most assertiveness. The smaller, more petty disagreements instead are the ones in which we tend to lose the most conversational footing with others. When we have a weak will and are only half committed to solving a problem is when we get ourselves into the most trouble here. These more minuscule issues do make up the bulk of our conflicts over time, though, so focusing on solving these are the most surefire way of resolving our issues with others across the board.

In public, we tend to be at our least assertive. It is amazing the things that people will put up with in others out of fear of losing face in public. However, public spheres are where we find more of our interpersonal conflicts so practicing assertiveness in public is another great way to lessen our overall conflict anxiety.

Restaurants are great breeders of interpersonal conflict; there are just so many things going on within a confined space and so many wires being crossed as a result. Here we have a great opportunity to practice assertiveness where it is needed most: in noisy, confusing, and shambolic situations.

Let's say that a person waits for half an hour on a plate at a restaurant. He or she could react with passivity, assertiveness, passive aggressiveness, or aggressiveness. Passivity here would entail simply ignoring the problem and trusting the food to arrive whenever it happens to do so, and not telling any servers or managers about the problem. This avoidance only makes conflict anxiety worse with the passage of time and does not necessarily lead to the customer getting what he or she wants. The passive aggressive solution would there be to address the conflict indirectly, perhaps by complaining to another customer or by reviewing the place negatively online. This is not a valid overall solution because, like the first, this one still does not necessarily get the food to come. An aggressive approach would be to start screaming at all the waiters, which is obviously not helpful. An assertive person would handle this problem calmly and directly, pulling a waiter aside and asking him or her respectfully why the food is such a long time coming. It is only the assertive solution that here solves the problem, as is the case in most situations.

Haggling and bargaining are two other areas in which assertiveness is key. In order to haggle effectively, we must first have some knowledge of the appropriate price range of what we are purchasing is. This will make our offers more realistic and easier to be agreed upon. Seeing what other people pay for items and agreeing to pay no more is one great way to ascertain marketplace value on items. Once we have gained some concept of this value, we can then think of our preferred prices. Here we can use percentages to our advantage; asking for 50% of an item's retail cost and then meeting the retailer halfway at around 75% is one of the greatest methods we can use here.

The definition of common knowledge in game theory is the endless loop of our own awareness of the awareness of others, followed by their awareness of our own awareness, and so on and so forth. When haggling, we should establish some sense of common knowledge with the seller, indicating that we know just as much as they do and that they know just as much as we do. Doing things that indicate this level of common knowledge, such as responding frankly to prices that are either too high or too low, will put us on an even platform with those who we haggle with.

Once we have this even platform established, we can finally negotiate from a position of strength and knowledge rather than one of weakness and ignorance. Assertive offers that are within our budgets can be made once we have allowed that we have to work within the boundaries of common knowledge. Here no nonassertive modes of conduct will land us the deals that we are desirous of because these modes are seen right through by people who are trying to protect their finances.

We lack assertiveness most when we find ourselves caught off guard or stressed out the most. When we are surprised, we tend to lose the ability to communicate what we are thinking clearly. We can be caught off guard in positive, negative, or neutral ways, but whatever the circumstances happen to be, we always seem to lose some communication abilities when blind sighted by new happenings.

We are usually blind sighted more by negative happenings than by any other kinds. Not only are we typically not met with pleasant surprises, but assertiveness is not in order when these pleasantries come about, so here we will focus solely on the shock caused by unfortunate turns of events. Before asserting ourselves in more dire situations, we have to determine what it is exactly that we should be asserting. Here we cannot let our instantaneous emotions and reactions cloud our faculty of judgment.

Speaking on idioms, being put on the spot is another easy way to lose assertiveness. This is similar to being caught off guard in that it gives us the same feelings of discomfort and confusion. The main difference between being caught off guard and being put on the spot is, however, that there is some sort of attention necessarily being paid to us when we are put on the spot. We can, as a matter of fact, be both though. Sometimes we are faced with situations in which we have to act spontaneously in front of others. Speaking deliberately becomes difficult in these situations in which we have to act fast in front of others.

When we are put on the spot, it is usually because no one else in the given situation knows exactly what to say or do, so any number or all of them look to us for some kind of direction as to what to do next. We are also put on the spot when faced with difficult questions from others. This usually occurs around additional people, who may or may not know us and or the details of what we are being asked about. In either case, being put on the spot is uncomfortable and stressful, and is often dealt with in ungainly and sometimes zany ways.

When we are put on the spot by others because they want us to in some way lead them, we should take this as a compliment. If we are being seen as being knowledgeable by others, we should try to act the part, even if it is not fully in line with our character, as the situation suggests. In these situations, we can either admit our ignorance or assert whatever it is that we happen to know. Both of these options are valid because performing them is within the honest boundaries of our intellect. Another option that would not be valid and would lead to hardships and tribulations would be to lie, or at least fictionalize, about our own merits and claim to know more about what is going on than we in fact do. Everyone does this from time to time, whether they realize it or not. We try to bolster our image in the eyes of our observers by biting off more than we can chew in accusations and assertions when we like those who are observing us. This is, however, always seen through as being the charade it truly is because people can only be put off of the truth about us for so long before looking into the topics on which we speak for themselves.

We can also be put on the spot by accusations and questions from others. We will virtually always do well to respond to these inquiries honestly and straightforwardly unless we allow for ourselves "little white lies" that serve to keep the mood of the situation light and comfortable, a concession which is not made by all but does arguably have ethical benefits to offer. When these questions turn to accusations is when we should focus on asserting ourselves and showing that we are not guilty of anything and that our accusers may or may not be exceeding the boundaries' truth holds over them. There are also, of course, allegations with intimations that are unassailable, and we should treat these as they are so as to never appear dishonest ourselves among others.

We have to keep in mind that we are limited in what we can do when eyes are turned onto us. We are limited not only in our own abilities but also in how much we can appease or even affect others. Assertiveness in these scenarios is best spent towards our concerted efforts at making the situation better for ourselves, not towards pleasing other people. We should take any unnecessary attention that we are given, as an opportunity to further our own self-interests by expressing how we truly feel, rather than using this attention to try to get others to admire or even agree with us. Working calmly towards our own ends will drown out much of the superfluous noise generated by others in times of stress.

We can be put on the spot in any number of the places that we find ourselves in, including workplace environments. When we are pressured in this way at work, it is usually because someone else wants something out of us. Rather than letting the apparent urgency of the request overwhelm us and force us to comply, we should take a second to consider what we can and cannot do, or better, what we should and should not do. This will put the power into our own hands as to what we are going to work on. Sometimes we get orders from superiors that are simply out of our reach, ones that have to be rejected. If we manage to reject these orders in a calm and respectful way, asserting that they are truly out of our powers and that we would be better off doing something else, then we are bound to be met with much less resistance and frustration, perhaps even none at all.

Public speaking is another area of life in which most people experience lots of discomforts. Words mean everything to people, so it comes as no surprise that people tend to get in their heads about what they have to say in front of crowds of people. There is usually no telling who we are going to be speaking to when speaking publicly. While this fact can be anxiety provoking, it can also be helpful in that it eliminates any perceived need to cater to or to please any specific type of person. There is a paradox of overexposure and anonymity in public speech, overexposure in that lots of people see the faces of public speakers, and anonymity in that the speaker chooses what he or she has to say.

The best way to deal with public speaking anxiety is through exposure therapy: getting out into the world and speaking up in front of any random people we choose. Taking measures to "get out of our bodies" is another great step to take. There is no need to worry about what we look like so long as the content of our speech is deliberate and edited as we and only we see fit.

The fear of being caught off guard, being put on the spot, and of public speaking all have the same source: the overarching fear of being the center of attention. Not everyone likes the spotlight, which is most likely a good thing. It would be somewhat haughty even to have the desire of being observed all of the time. We should not let our fear of attention govern our lives, though. Instead, we should see the more uncomfortable situations in which there are lots of eyes on us as opportunities to express what we truly think and feel, and to push towards our personal goals with the help and support of those who are listening to us behind us.

There are also negative emotions that can hinder our assertiveness regardless of the experiences that we find ourselves having. These emotions usually much more destructive than mere external circumstances because our happiness and well-being are more dependent upon our faculties of imagination than they are on reason or external experience. We should go over how to deal with destructive emotions so that handling more uncomfortable situations will come with greater ease.

Worry/ nervousness

These are two of the most unpleasant and unhealthy emotions on the spectrum, and, unfortunately for workers, these two plagues virtually every workplace. This anxiety can stem from a number of sources: fear of getting laid off, social problems, low salaries, large workload, Etc, And be compounded with problems at home, or with family or friends by many. A small amount of stress can be a productive thing, but once it becomes chronic anxiety, health problems start to occur. Here are some tips on how to avoid excessive anxiety:

Break cycles of worry

Do not Surround yourself with anxiety. If you can foresee needless anxiety stemming from a situation or a conversation, avoid that anxiety. Try to mini-mize the number of anxiety-inducing things that you have to deal with.

Try deep breathing exercises

These help primarily to slow down your breathing and heart rate. There are all sorts of different deep breathing exercises that you can learn about on the internet. For one, there is cyclical breathing, within breaths for 4 seconds followed by holding for 4 seconds, and then out breaths for 4 seconds followed by holding for 4 seconds. When doing these exercises, it is important to focus on your breathing and nothing else. In addition to these exercises, there are other physical relaxation exercises that will help reduce workplace stress, including progressive muscle relaxation.

Focus on improving the situation

Whatever it is worrying you with regard to work, brainstorming solutions and making attempts at them will help reduce your anxiety greatly. Doing these things will also make you a more valuable asset to your company.

Journal your worries down

Simply writing down the things that bother, you will do a lot to alleviate the anxiety surrounding them. This technique also helps to curtail sleep problems and nightmares, as worries that we write down during the day don't typically bother us by night. Once these are written down, you can then schedule times to deal with these issues. Before that time comes, let these issues leave you and go about your day. When that time comes, make sure to perform proper risk analysis before putting any plans into place.

Worry and nervousness can decrease self-confidence and lead to health complications. it is always important to trail these negative emotions away and remain confident and secure.

Frustration/irritation

Frustration is more often than not caused by the feeling of being trapped or stuck at a point which you want to get out of, but can not. This feeling can be caused by a number of things, especially at work. A colleague blocking a project of yours, a boss too disorganized to catch a meeting on time, or a phone call held out longer than necessary are just a few examples that come to mind. Frustration, whatever its causes, should always be dealt with quickly because when it is not, it can accumulate into anger and other even more negative emotions.

There are, however, many ways of dealing with this awful emotion, a few of which are listed below:

- Stopping to evaluate

  The best thing to do when feelings of frustration arise is to stop what you are doing and take time to evaluate them. Writing your frustrations down in this stage can help very much. After this is done, think of some positive aspects of your current situation. This will improve your mood and reduce further frustration.

- Look for positive things

  Again, finding silver linings in a frustrating situation will make you see the events unfolding in a new light. This change in your thinking will improve your mood, among other things. If it is a person who is causing you frustration, then keep in mind that it is probably not personal, and if it is an event or situation, then it can probably be solved. Try to move on from this step as much as possible.

- Recall the last time you felt frustrated

If you can remember the last thing that you were frustrated about, then you can probably remember how that thing eventually resolved itself. Looking at things with hindsight, they always work out fine. You can also probably recall that your feelings of frustration did not do much to help you in that last situation, so to assume that they are helping you this time around would not be very prudent. Perspective is everything, and so many issues lose so much of their stature when seen through different angles.

Dislike

Dislike for certain coworkers is inevitable, and when it pops up, it seldom goes away. We all have to work with people who we dislike at one point or another, so when these people arrive, it is important to take steps towards dealing with them responsibly. Some of the best things that you can do in these situations are to:

- Show respect

  You are never obligated to get along with everyone you work with, but you are, in many ways, obligated to show them all respect. When these situations arise, pride and ego are two things which you should set aside, even if the other party(s) are not willing to. This will allow you to come out of the experience with your dignity intact, whatever the outcomes may be.

- Be assertive

  If a coworker is rude or unprofessional with you,

do not be afraid to tell them so. If you do so with certainty and fairness, they might be inclined to change some of their attitudes and behaviors in the future.

Anger/aggravation

Anger is arguably the most destructive emotion contained in a human. This is especially true when the anger is out of control in the workplace. It is also an emotion which most of us do not handle very well. As far as work is concerned, there is typically very little room for anger, which is problematic because much of it then gets taken home with us. Controlling this emotion is one of the most important steps in keeping any given job, especially for those who have difficulties with this. Some tips in dealing with this emotion are listed below:

- Watch for the early signs of anger

  No one else can detect when your anger is building up quite as you can, so detecting it early is your own responsibility. As was mentioned before, you decide how to react to situations, so if you react in anger, no one holds accountability for that happening.

- When anger arises, take a break from what you are doing

When you start to get angry, closing your eyes and trying the aforementioned deep breathing exercises can help you hugely. These actions will do a lot to interrupt your angry thoughts and help to put your mind back on a more positive, relaxed pathway, reducing irrational statements and decisions made.

- Picture yourself when you get angry

Imagining how you look and behave will usually give you some well-needed perspective on the situation at hand. For example, if you have the urge to shout at a coworker, think about what you would look like doing so: flustered, mean, and demanding. With that imagery in mind, it is easy to see that you would not be a good coworker in making that decision.

Disappointment/unhappiness

Disappointment and unhappiness are two of the more pullulated emotions in modern workplaces. These two are almost equal to anger in their unhealthiness; in fact, unhappiness may be more unhealthy. These can also have detrimental impacts on your productivity, as they can leave you feeling exhausted and drained, and also less inclined to take risks in the future. Here are some steps that can be taken to curtail the effects of these awful emotions:

- Consider your mindset

  Try to always keep in mind that things will not always go your way. If they did, then life would become prosaic and meaningless. It is, sometimes, the adversity and the suffering that give life its meat. Do not try to avoid these things; the answer to these problems lies within the willingness to confront them.

- Set and adjust your goals

  Disappointment can often stem from neglecting to reach a goal. This rarely means, however, that the goal is no longer reachable though. It is natural to feel disappointment in these situations, but you must always find the willpower to pick yourself back up. You could, for example, keep your goal, but just make a small change. Anything that will help you to get past the disappointments that you face.

- Record your thoughts

  One method for dealing with negative emotions is to write them down. When you feel unhappy or disappointed, try writing down what is bothering you, and be specific about your concerns. Is it your job that is bothering you? A coworker? Do you have too heavy of a workload? Writing these concerns down will help you to single out what exactly is bothering you and how you can improve on these areas of concern. Remember that you always have more powers than you think in improving a situation.

- Remember to smile

  Forcing a smile onto your face can actually make you feel happier and relieve stress. In addition, this activity also releases the neurotransmitters' dopamine, endorphins, and serotonin, which all lower heart rate and blood pressure. The endorphins released also act as natural painkillers, and the serotonin acts as a natural antidepressant. Smiling will also make you look more attractive to those around you, further bettering the relationships you have with your coworkers.

Now that the main emotions that have adverse effects on most workers have been covered, let's take a look at some more strategies of dealing with these:

Compartmentalize your stressors

Try to keep stress and baggage from work and home in those respective places. You can use mental techniques, such as imagining the stressors locked away in a box for the time being. If you do not try to compartmentalize these issues, then waters will get very muddied up in your personal life, and things will become very complicated.

Identify your own self-talk

Relay to yourself what you tell yourself. By doing this, you may find yourself repeating thoughts and phrases to yourself that are not necessarily true or helpful. Try to identify your own thoughts that may be misleading or based on thinking errors. Doing this will help you move on from some of your worse points and attitudes into a more productive and expansive mindset.

Identify and accept your emotion

There is virtually nothing you can do to control an emotion that you are not even willing to come to terms with having. It is like denying the existence of a spider right in front of your eyes; the spider will just get bigger and bigger until it is all that you can see. In identifying what emotion(s) you are having and accepting that they are a natural part of life, you are taking lots of power away from them. In doing this, you are also becoming a greater solver of your own problems.

Affirm your rights

There are many places in life, work especially, where you are bound to feel like you have no rights and no control over what happens to you. By identifying your rights and your powers, you are giving yourself some perspective on the things that are in and out of your control. After taking some time to do this, you may find that you are much more powerful than you think you are. This will improve your mood and your self-confidence to affirm these rights that you have.

Communicate strategically

Anyone can drone on about the things that they do not like, but it takes skill and grit actually to get things done to fix all their problems. When you are trying to communicate with others, especially disagreements, It is always important to be precise in your language. This will allow you to communicate your qualms more effectively, and it will also decrease the chance of having misunderstandings and heated arguments. When trying to get the point across, try to come into the situation with some idea of what you want to get accomplished, and your probability of having a productive conversation will increase dramatically. If others reply emotionally, let them vent and be understanding. You may learn more from them than they will from you. Ask for more details as well, and the two of you will probably come closer to an understanding because of it.

Be objective

Try to look at whatever is bothering you from both analytic and synthetic approaches. An analytic approach will help you understand the one issue more in depth and with more clarity, while a synthetic approach will help you understand the issue within the class of all of your possible issues. It is important to look into things with depth and focus, but seeing things as parts of your whole understanding will help you to make connections and find out why these certain things bother you through free associations.

Emotions are never right or wrong, they are only felt. There is no shame in feeling emotions unless of course, the emotion is shame. Emotions will always come and go and are always wiser than the ego. Each one of us, however, has free will in how we react to life's vicissitudes. Controlling emotions is not always easy, in fact, sometimes it becomes nearly impossible. But this skill is just like any other in that it can be improved with practice and diligence.

How To Bring Inner-Assertiveness To Outward Action

All the assertiveness training in the world will go to waste in one who will not take the steps actually to act assertively out in the world. Here is where those who know how to be assertive, theoretically are separated from actually assertive people. Assertive people will actually take measures to assert themselves out in the world, while others will usually think of assertive things to say pertaining situations they find themselves in and never actually voice these more polarizing opinions to others. It does not matter how fair or unfair we happen to be with others within our own internal monologues if we do not take the step of voicing our opinions come to within these dialogues to others. To simply think assertively and to never act assertively is to hit the bulls-eye on the wrong target; if we are going to better our situation in life, we are going to have actually to express ourselves freely.

We all have certain personal boundaries, positions, needs, and wants. These are cued up in our minds at all times, almost begging to be expressed at any given moment. The basic and most fundamental problem of non-assertiveness is the avoidance of this direct expression. This avoidance will invariably choke us off from our own aspirations if we allow it to.

We know that the avoidance of the expression of boundaries, positions, needs, and wants are the most common cause of non-assertiveness. We could even consider this avoidance synonymous with non-assertiveness, thought the two concepts are different from one another. The nonassertive person does not push his or her own agenda in social situations as a result of this habit of pushing the expression of these stances aside. While the temporary avoidance of these expressions is needed in order to edit our thoughts at times properly, long term avoidance can cause a person's stances to lose visibility over time. This can help one to cover one's own intellectual trail and to adapt his or her beliefs without the interjections of others, but it usually only serves to frustrate and alienate those who avoid in this way.

Temporary avoidance of expression is sometimes a rational route to take through moral and intellectual tribulations, but there should always be a fine balance maintained between over and under speaking. It could be said about assertiveness what Will Durant said about genius: that it is half knowledge, half tact. We can choose not to express the viewpoints that we are less sure of, as well as the ones that we are sure of, but do not feel, are pertinent. Not everything that we think and feel is going to seem purposive to others, which is fine. Another one of Will Durant's gems of wisdom could be applied here: To say nothing, especially when speaking, is half the art of diplomacy.

Now we are aware that not all of our opinions need to be voiced, and that we are the only ones legislating what is and is not said by us. The only ground to cover at this point is what we should express. This is, of course, subjective and discursive, but there are certain personal things that we all feel need to be expressed above all others. The subjectivity of what we feel should be expressed by us is due to the fact that a stance that we take up has to meet a set of criteria, one that is only determined by our own power of understanding, working largely unconsciously. This set of criteria is contingent and indeterminate, incessantly being edited and updated by our faculty of judgment's variable purposiveness. This variable purposiveness presupposes that we are never exactly sure of the truth behind matters, but the solution that assertive modes of conduct provide is found in our assertions of apparent truths that can be communicated and further constructed through dialogues with others.

If the indetermination and apparent flimsiness of our viewpoints deter us from expressing ourselves and operating functionally within society, then we can take refuge in the fact that no one else has any determinate or even necessarily accurate conceptualization of what truth really is. It is not those who are necessarily more intelligent or more in line with reality who are listened to the most. Instead, the people who take action and make their voices heard openly are paid the most attention to. Whenever we choose to speak on matters, there exist entire collections of possible variable scenarios. Within these scenarios, there is little correlation between the apparent truth behind what an individual is saying and how the message is being interpreted by others. Observers within a crowd have their own sets of criteria published by their own powers of understanding, so if someone disagrees with the message another lays forth, there is little that the speaker can or even should do to advance his or her opinion in the mind's eye of the disagreeing observer.

The most overwhelming proponent of assertiveness is the concept of free speech itself. With free speech, we can simply say whatever we choose to anyways, so long as we do not threaten others. With this fundamental right granted to us, we lose any rational justification for social anxiety altogether.

Knowing that we are at once free to edit what we choose to say and also free to say virtually whatever we want to, we take a head start into conversations that give us the confidence to make any claims and express any observations that we choose to. With this knowledge of our personal freedoms concerning speech rights, we will now delve into how to better assert ourselves practically in the real world.

Body language is a great indication of assertiveness. Assertive people tend to have fuller posture overall, usually walking and standing with their backs straight up and their shoulders rolled back, and with their chests protruding outwards. This is the posture that projects the most confidence in a person and that one that indicates the highest status among people. Eye contact is another great indicator of confidence or diffidence, depending on its length within a given scenario. People who are more confident usually make a natural and "normal" amount of eye contact, while diffident people usually either gaze too long or do not look up at other's eyes at all. The most confident possible way in which to speak to another person is to posture correctly and to maintain healthy eye contact.

The tone of voice should also be paid attention to. We tend to break rapport and inflict our voices downward when speaking to inferiors at work or people who we do not feel threatened by/ do not want to be around. Rapport seeking is when we end our phrases with upward inflections with the (usually subconscious) aim at appeasing or impressing those who we are speaking with. To be rapport neutral is to speak with a steady tone of voice, one that does not indicate an attempt to please or to displease those who we are speaking with. Finally, there is a monotone tone of voice, which features no inflections whatsoever and does not indicate any expression as a result.

The use of assertive modes of conduct is typically associated with instances of conflict, though these modes are also applicable and appropriate in times of peace. Assertiveness is not caused by, nor is the cause of, conflict when we are simply stating opinions as they stand in times of peace. This type of assertiveness could be called theoretical rather than practical because it consists of simply stating the facts as we perceive them rather than willing purposive action.

While theoretical assertiveness can be used to assert our opinions on non-divisive issues, practical assertiveness is arguably more useful in that it allows us to take potentially more controversial stances on issues that we may care about more. This utility is not correlated with the controversiality of the subject matter but is correlated to our willingness to oppose others on the premise that those who can oppose others are more potent actors, and with this potency, they gain utility.

Practical assertiveness should be practiced, especially when we have some sort of obstacle that stands in between our current selves and our goals. We can assert ourselves regarding peripheral issues as well, but these assertions have less utility in that they concern issues that affect us less. With that being said, it is clarified that we should prioritize issues that stand in our way over those that do not. For example, if a person is concerned about both a bad relationship at work and the details of an investigation concerning unknown people at once, he or she will probably reap more benefit from spending an evening out with the coworker in question than from spending the same evening following the investigation. We are usually not capable of solving both direct and more peripheral issues at once. With this fact in mind, we should limit our areas of concern to what directly affects us rather than flustering ourselves with aloof issues.

Practical assertions come in many forms, all having their own unique purposes and ends. Some of the most common forms of practical assertions are accusations, inquiries, corrections, demands, and propositions. The basis of a practical assertion is practicality, so we will say here that all practical assertions subsume a purposiveness. This purposiveness does not imply a purpose, or at least a determinate purpose, because we can make practical assertions without necessarily having an end goal in mind. These assertions do still subsume a purposiveness because they are practical and directional in their nature.

Practical assertions in the form of accusations or allegations are initiated by a perceived practice of an action or behavior, usually coupled with the presupposition that the action or behavior is negative or divergent from the accuser's conceptualization of righteous conduct. Here accusers assert that the accused have performed some sort of action or behavior. Some accusations turn out to be true and others false, just as some accusers believe their claims to be true and others simply lie. Usually, accusers believe the veracity of their claims and attempt to make the accused parties either confirm or deny their suspicions.

When we are accused of something, we should review our rights and the details of the subject matter at hand before responding. Doing so with honesty will keep us from falling into the traps of malevolent people, or unintentionally misleading our accusers. When we are wrongfully accused of something, we should express that we have been wrongfully accused. Here we also maintain the right to detach ourselves peacefully from our accusers, allowing ourselves to be influenced by them as we and only we deem appropriate.

There are also situations in which we have to act as the accuser. Before doing so, we have to carefully analyze our assertions, pouring over the truth of the allegation, and determining the veracity in our own claims. If we feel that we need to accuse another of something, then we should do so as soon as we are certain that our accusations are grounded in truth. Here we should avoid attacking the character of the accused and instead respectfully stick to what we believe they have done and why we may feel negative about it. This should be done as pragmatically as possible, with attention paid only to the details that affect us most directly.

Practical assertions in the form of inquiries are similar to accusations and allegations but do not have the same negative connotation. These assertions are in between proclamations and questions. We usually find these when we are discussing the details of something and are only half sure of what these details really are. An inquiry usually does not take on an accusation tone but does have the same will to veracity that an accusation does. These also differ from accusations in their subject matter; we usually only accuse people but can inquire into anything.

Corrections are arguably the most useful assertions because they serve to keep truths consistent among parties. Usually, those correcting others believe themselves to be in the right, though there are cases in which people mislead others; these case could not be called corrections though, they are simply lies, which could be another type of assertion. Without the willingness to correct others when we deem doing so appropriate, we lose our ability to accurately determine the veracity in what others say to us. While we can silently correct others inwardly, these corrections never seem as valid to us because part of ourselves wonders why we were afraid to voice the stance in the first place.

When we are corrected by others, we should give them the benefit of the doubt, meaning we should trust their judgment and the honesty in their assertion, but we should also take what they have to say with a certain degree of skepticism and determine whether their correction is appropriate. There is no need to be put off by a correction. These types of assertions should usually be taken as conveyances that we are granted so that we can think more accurately in the future.

It is in correcting others that we usually have more difficulty. When we do so, we should make sure that our corrections are valid ones that lead to the truth, and proceed to make our assertions respectfully with the intent of bettering overall knowledge rather than of chastising others. Secure people will be grateful when we correct them. As for insecure people, our corrections will still yield utility overall, though they may be met with more resistance.

Demands are unique among other forms of practical assertions in that they place certain parties in highly subordinate roles. The role of the demanded is a much more limited one than other roles brought about by other practical assertions. A demand is a sort of unnegotiated (and sometimes nonnegotiable) request that we can ask of others.

When demanding others, we have to keep their own autonomy in mind to the degree to which we would prefer that they did the same for us. By this categorical imperative, we can make demands with whatever degree of audacity that we see fit (i.e., the amount of audacity that we would tolerate in others making demands for us). This amount would follow a set of criteria that our power of understanding would impose upon itself. When we are demanded by others, we should ascertain whether or not we are able to meet said demands and whether meeting these demands would benefit ourselves, and base our decisions accordingly.

Finally, a proposition is a practical assertion that communicates an idea or a concept to others, usually proposed with the intention of meeting a certain end. These can also be made to solve problems and are usually meant to be beneficial to all parties involved. Without a certain degree of assertiveness, we are never likely to put forth propositions and are prone to accept those of others without considering our own self-interests.

Chapter Six

Techniques For Everyday Conversations

A 'first impression' technically consists of the first seven seconds, which elapse when you first meet a person. This is undoubtedly the most important time spent with another person, which will make or break the quality of the relationship. This is why it is important to act fast when meeting a new person and make sure that they do not come out of this all-important time allotment with a bad taste in their mouths. To ensure that you have little difficulty in making new relationships in the future, here are a few tips in making first impressions:

Smile

Facial expressions are one of the most important factors in making first impressions. By starting a relationship off with a smile, you are associating yourself with positivity. 48 percent of Americans claim that a person's smile becomes their most memorable trait after meeting them. Sometimes excessive smiling can seem unauthentic or even arrogant but smiling authentically always tends to charm.

Not only does smiling make good first impressions more accessible, but it also is shown to decrease levels of stress hormones such as cortisol and adrenaline. Smiling is not only friendly, but it is also one of the main keys to longevity.

Give a good handshake

A proper handshake remains one of the tenants of politeness the world over. Giving a good one, however, depends on maintaining that important balance between being too firm and too soft. If a healthy medium is established, then you will make much better first impressions.

Give a good introduction

Verbal introductions are the most important part of the first seven seconds spent with someone. There are plenty of common introductions in our vernacular; these include 'hello,' 'nice to meet you,' etc. Whichever one you use, a verbal introduction can help very much to break the silence and tension involved in meeting someone new.

Enunciate clearly

A common issue that lots of people are confronted with in meeting new people is that they lack the confidence to speak clearly. Speaking timidly is not only an easy way to be overlooked but it also often leads to being taken less seriously. It has been shown that those who speak in a deeper and calmer voice are usually taken more seriously, so find a balance between whispering and screaming, and you will tend to create better relationships.

Maintain eye contact

Eye contact shows others that you are not only interested in what they are saying, but that you are also confident in yourself. Eye contact is also a great indicator of respect among people. It is, however, to be used in moderation though. Too much eye contact can intimidate a person or make them feel uncomfortable, while looking away may be construed as a distraction.

Use welcoming body language

Body language is, more often than not, mirrored when two people are talking to one another. Your smile, for example, is mirrored by those around you by means of a specialized neuron responsible for mirroring facial expressions. This establishes between the two of you, mutual understanding, connection, and trust. Other usages of positive body language are helpful as well, especially when carried out within the first seven seconds of meeting a new person.

Dress nicely

Your attire can be a huge indicator of what you are like to a new person. If you dress in clothes that make you feel comfortable and confident, people are more likely to perceive you as being that way. The opposite, however, is also true. Not only will dress well help you to make better first impressions, but it will also improve your mood and your confidence.

Commit names to memory

In the words of Dale Carnegie, "We should be aware of the magic contained in a name and realize that this single item is wholly and completely owned by the person with whom we are dealing and nobody else." People very much enjoy hearing their own names, even more so than they usually realize. Hearing one's own name can especially stick out to people in the modern era, which is so overwhelming in its excess of names and information. Once you remember someone's name, it is always a good idea to keep calling that person by their name as this you make you seem more agreeable.

Consider your own intentions

This is an aspect of life that people tend to neglect. Ask yourself what your own goals are in meeting any given new person. A clear vision of what these goals might be will give you more of an idea of how to set your tone and behave around this person. This will also make it much easier to communicate with others because you will have a better idea of what you are communicating.

Project thoughtfulness

No one wants to talk to a person who is not interested in what they have to say or who does not think before he or she speaks. This is why it is important to err on the side of viewing others as potential teachers and also to be precise in what you have to say. It will make others more inclined to want to talk to you if you show empathy for them and try to give them only the best of what you have to say. Showing thoughtfulness in your words or actions is one of the best ways of making a lasting impression on others.

Avoid projecting your bad moods

Bad moods can make unexpectedly strong impressions on people. If you are meeting a new person but are in a bad mood for whatever reason, try your hardest to leave your negativity behind you. It is always amazing how easily negative attitudes can rub off on others around you.

Answer questions with grace

The way a person handles being questioned is often a great indicator of their overall character. People who either get too defensive or yield at once when combated with questions are usually put under further scrutiny. This is because they can come across as being insecure or dishonest. The way you handle being questioned is going to be analyzed carefully by those who you come into contact with, so knowing how to react when questioned is very useful.

Try to answer all questions that you are faced with in a practical, straightforward manner and whenever you do not have a good answer to someone's question, try using the same strategy that many politicians use under these circumstances, answer a different but related question. Another important piece of advice is to not take questions as personal attacks, instead, take them as indicators of the interest that other people have in you.

Practice and prepare

Like any other types of skills, communication skills take lots of practice to master. You can not expect to have every meeting or encounter that you are faced with to go well at first. It is only after you have taken the initiative to meet lots of new people that you will get better with first impressions. This tip is especially useful for shy or timid people. If you are shy and do not like meeting new people, then the only way to develop this skill is to practice it. You should to introducing yourself to a new person every week to start out with, and you will see your interpersonal skills develop dramatically.

Project confidence

It is natural to feel apprehensive when you are meeting a new person who you do not know anything about. In these situations, it becomes important to keep in mind that this other person is probably just an average man or woman. In other words, you are probably not dealing with a famous astrophysicist or rapper. Remaining cognizant of this will help to take lots of unnecessary pressure off of you. When you do feel anxious in these situations, try your hardest not to let your anxiety show. One of the easiest ways to project confidence when speaking to people are to lower your voice and keep a calm, even tone. This will put your listeners at ease and make even them more confident in what you are saying.

While there are many ways to ensure that you are making a good first impression, there are also a number of ways to destroy any chance of making one. These mistakes are commonly made by even the most polite among us and often leave new people we meet not wanting to talk to us again. Here are some of the most detrimental things that you can do when meeting a new person:

Aiming to keep calm waters rather than setting boundaries

Situations will inevitably arise when you are forced to set boundaries with people. In these situations, whether they be with someone who you are meeting for the first time or someone you have known for a while, it is important to find an assertive balance between screaming at another person and politely laughing off the disrespect, aggression, or even abuse that you are receiving. Taking measures to set boundaries is especially important in work and or family situations, where you may wind up knowing the person in question for a long time. If one party has no parameters to follow when speaking to a party that won't put its foot down, then relationships are only going to deteriorate. While setting boundaries may be uncomfortable or put others off, it is worth it in the long run as it will establish your esteem and make you more comfortable.

Avoiding differences and looking only at commonalities

It is now clear within the psychological sciences that people tend to look for and enjoy things that are similar to them. While this is understandable, it also tends to lead to people neglecting to notice the differences between others and themselves and only looking into similarities. This is not a good habit to get into because it neglects potentially valuable information regarding another person's views, beliefs, etc. Recognizing the disagreements that you have with another person at their onset will not only set up some additional boundaries, but it will also build trust between you and the other person because there is an assurance that nothing is being left unearthed between the two of you.

The phrase 'fake it 'till you make' applies only to body and nonverbal language

You have to be honest in what you say. This is probably the most important tip that you will find within this chapter, if not this book. If you come into a conversation projecting confidence that you do not have, or, on the other hand, trying to play dumb, then people will tend to see right through you. If, however, you are honest and straightforward about your ideas, thoughts, and emotions, then people will take what you say at face value, and they will gain respect and maybe even admiration for you. Being honest with others and yourself is the easiest and most natural way to be. It takes far more effort to lie than it does just, to tell the truth, and telling the truth will always yield better results in the long run.

The tone of voice, as we all can tell, tends to expose more of the speaker's true feelings than the actual words spoken themselves often do. It serves to strip away the outer casings of a person's personality usually put up in common speech. The tone of voice is, for this reason, often the best and most reliable way of more clearly communicating our greater personality at large. The way that you or others use the tone of voice communicates a lot of how the speaker truly feels about the message being displayed, and it also has profound impacts of how listeners are going to receive the message.

When analyzing the tone of voice, there is a very broad and all-encompassing framework that you can use as a reference that consists of four different dimensions. We will now discuss these dimensions and their characteristics to get a better perspective on what to look out for when others speak to you.

There are obviously a nearly infinite amount of tones of voice and an even wider range of ways to interpret all of these, so categorization and dimension are useful tools in dealing with the multiplicity of all these tones.

The first dimension of the tone of voice is seriousness vs. funniness.

Regardless of subject matter, whether the speaker is trying to be funny or serious can tell you a lot about the greater situation at hand and or the speaker's personality. If the tone is a funny one, then you could infer that the speaker is a rather tongue in cheek person who likes to have a good time and keep things light-hearted, or that he or she is in a cheerful mood. If the tone is a serious one, then you could infer that the speaker is something of a straightforward and practical person, if not unfriendly or boring, or that he or she is in a more serious mood. Analyzing this dimension of speech can not only give you insights into the speaker's character, but it can also give you a better grasp on how to go about talking to him or her or how to deal with the situation at hand. This can lead to better communication and potential problem-solving.

The second dimension of the tone of voice is causality vs. formality.

Regardless of subject matter, whether the speaker is remaining casual or formal can indicate a lot of things about the greater situation at hand and or the speaker's personality. If the tone is a casual one, then you could infer that the speaker is a rather casual and down to earth person who likes to keep things comfortable and maybe a bit more laid back, or that the speaker is in a more casual or comfortable mood at the time. If, on the other hand, the tone of voice is more of a formal one, then you could infer that the speaker is a more formal person who prefers to keep things more impersonal and professional, or that the speaker is in a more serious, formal mood. Noticing whether the speaker is taking on a more casual tone of voice or a more formal one can give you a good indication of how to better communicate with him or her, and it could even give you some insights into his or her character.

The third dimension of the tone of voice is irreverence vs. respectfulness.

Regardless of subject matter, whether the speaker is more irreverent in his or her tone or more respectful can indicate a lot of things about the greater situation at hand and or the speaker's personality. If the tone is more of an irreverent one, then you can infer that the speaker may not have very much respect for you and or the subject matter at hand, or-then again-he or she may just be in a bad or irreverent mood. If, on the other hand, the tone of voice used is a more respectful one, then you may infer that the speaker is a more respectful person and values treating others with dignity more, or that he or she is in a more righteous and respectful mood than the other speaker. Noticing whether the tone of voice is a more irreverent or a more respectful one can give you a good indication of how to communicate with the speaker, and it could even give you some insights into his or her character.

And finally, the fourth dimension of the tone of voice is a matter of facts vs. enthusiasm.

It should first be noted that these two are not mutually exclusive as there are some instances where genuine enthusiasm is understandable. Regardless of subject matter, whether the speaker is more matter of fact in his or her tone or more enthusiastic can a lot of things about the greater situation at hand and or the speaker's personality. If the tone happens to be a more matter of fact one, then you can infer that the speaker is a more matter of fact and straightforward person, or that he or she is just in a more practical mood. If, on the other hand, the tone is a more enthusiastic one, then you can infer that the speaker is an energetic and lively person, or that he or she is just in an enthusiastic mood. Noticing whether the tone of voice is a more matter of fact or a more enthusiastic one can give you a good indication of how to communicate with the speaker and it could even give you some insights into his or her character.

Chapter Seven

Realistic Examples Of Assertiveness In Dialogue

Now that we have established some boundaries and learned some techniques for assertive speech, we should learn how to apply these concepts within everyday dialogues. Not every example of assertive speech is destined to be met with rewarding results, so examples in which we will not get our way despite acting assertively will be included here.

Let's start off with some workplace scenarios, the scenarios most likely to call for assertive action. Let's say that a teacher works in a school with an intellectually impaired student. This teacher's name is Robert. Robert does not teach the student in question, and this student is instead taught by Linda. Linda's main strategy regarding teaching the student re-volves around keeping the student caught up with the rest of his classmates. Robert, on the other hand, would rather the student learn at a slower, more manageable pace, and would adjust his teaching style accordingly if he were the student's teacher.

Robert feels strongly that the student should be taught at a slower pace for the sake of clarity, while Linda feels strongly that the student should remain caught up with the others so as to avoid ostracism. This creates a conflict of interests between the two teachers, and an attempt to resolve this conflict is made by the principle, Mr. Shepard.

Robert and Linda meet with Mr. Shepard, and the first thing that Robert has to say concerning the mat-ter is: "Jordan (the student) should not be held to the same academic standard as the other students. These attempts at getting him caught up with the others are only causing problems. He is being rushed and not remembering the material as effectively as the others as a result. I think we should devise an academic plan for him that would be more suitable to his needs."

Linda replies: "Jordan is doing well in class. He has no missing assignments and has passed every test. He is just as smart as any of the other students, yet he is still singled out as the slow one. I think he is doing fine and will continue to do fine going at the same pace as all of the others. To hold him back would only make him feel more isolated and alienated."

Mr. Shepard sides with Linda and allows her to keep teaching Jordan at her own pace. Robert accepts Mr. Shepard's verdict without argument. He teaches the next day with no further interjections concerning the matter and does not carry his case on further.

Here we have a classic example of someone not getting his way even though he has chosen to make his argument in an assertive manner. Richard's subsequent decision to respect Mr. Shepard's authority and drop the argument is admirable and should be emulated by those who have acted assertively and still not met their ends. Here Richard shows us that some defeats should be met with humility and digression.

Let's take another example into account. Stephan, a judge, works in a courthouse with Jerry, a prosecutor. A case is brought up concerning Ethan, a man caught stealing food from a grocery store in an effort to feed his family. Stephan feels that since Ethan has no prior convictions on his record, he should be sentenced to community service rather than to any period of jail time. Jerry, on the other hand, knows Ethan through acquaintances and is convinced that he steals from grocery stores regularly and that he should be thrown in jail as a result. Ethan's case is brought before the court, and the dialogue between the judge and prosecutor goes as follows.

"Ethan is a habitual thief, and his account of the grocery store incident should not be trusted," says Jerry. "I have reason to believe that Ethan steals food on a regular basis and should be punished accordingly. I do not think that any length of community service will get him to change his ways. The only fitting punishment for Ethan would be jail time, as far as I am concerned."

Stephan responds: "While I remain convinced that Ethan did steal from the supermarket at the time in question, I have no reason to believe that he does not lead an otherwise lawful life. His actions, while illegal, were meant to sustain his family, and I cannot conceive that he would commit any similar acts in the future. I sentence Ethan to two weeks of community service."

At this point, Jeff remains silent and respectfully leaves the courtroom. Whether or not Jeff proceeds to keep an eye on Ethan is his own decision to make. What should be borrowed from Jeff regardless is his ability to keep his composure and respect the decision of the judge regardless of whether or not he agreed with said decision.

Now let's take an example of assertive speech translating into beneficial turns of events into account. Here Kanye, a foreign exchange student, is incensed by his neighbor Skylynn's habit of blaring music late at night and decides to confront her about the behavior.

"Skylynn, no one can sleep when you play your music so loudly," says Kanye. "You blare it into 4 or 5 a.m every morning, and it makes sleeping impossible. Our neighbors should not have to adapt to your schedule, but you are forcing us to. Please either keep it down or don't play it all throughout those hours."

To which Skylynn replies: "If my music is a problem for you, just put headphones in or turn on your own noise. I have a right to listen to what I want when I want."

"I'm not going to do either of those things," Kanye says. "You are causing a disturbance with what you are doing, and you have no right to bother others when they are trying to sleep. Stop blaring music, or I am going to call the police."

Skylynn then stops playing the music so early in the morning, and the conflict resolves itself. Kanye responded in the correct way here because he kept pushing on the matter because he knew that he was in the right legally. Here Kanye teaches us that assertiveness that crumbles as soon as one is contradicted is of limited use. Sometimes we have to continue to argue with others just to protect our rights.

We know now that assertive behavior pays off even when we do not get our way within a certain situation. While our needs may not always be met through assertive speech, these needs are expressed and worked towards more clearly through these more direct modes of conduct. Assertiveness in this respect is like a game, one that rewards persistence throughout all situations in which we deem its practice necessary. In other words, while assertiveness may not help us win all of our individual games, it will help us win the meta-game. In navigating the world with assertiveness, we are not guaranteeing wins, but are developing our capacities to deal with situations that we find adverse or disagreeable.

Regardless of the outcome, the use of assertiveness where we deem it appropriate is crucial to conversational skills. We simply cannot clearly express our perspectives without some degree of assertiveness.

CONCLUSION

Thank you for enjoying *Assertiveness Training: The complete workbook for women and men to learn outstanding assertiveness strategies. Change your behavior, stand up for yourself, and reap the benefits that will 10x your confidence.*

The areas that were covered within this book are as follows: How to stop lying to yourself and how to communicate how you feel towards others in your life, Inspiring confidence in yourself through assertiveness, Why we sometimes lack assertiveness, Maintaining assertiveness in uncomfortable situations, How to bring inner-assertiveness to outward action, Techniques for everyday conversations, and Realistic examples of assertiveness in dialogue.

No matter what your individual goals were in buying this book, hopefully you now have the information

you need to take it and turn it into actionable tools to become more assertive, and 10 your confidence anywhere and with anyone.
124

Good luck in all your future endeavors and never stop learning!

www.ingramcontent.com/pod-product-compliance
Lightning Source LLC
LaVergne TN
LVHW042204190726
843493LV00006B/1802